EXUMA DIAMAS REGN
(Book Four of the Exuma Infinite Series)

"...My Dear Daughter...I feel your hand in mine; your soul and mine blending, interdependent yet stronger together...and how limited are we really if our relationship continues to blossom, if we are communicating and embracing across the apparent divide of the dimensions - one in heavy, human clothes and the other dancing within an eternal body of elevated light - were it not for the daily grief in such a horrible tragedy of your youthful physical death, would I not see the growth towards total limitlessness as we walk together in this unbreakable bond...thus, the dimensions are one; all life unfolds in the timelessness of the present; we live this second truth in the crux of your elevation."

~ Kevin Mooney

Copyright 2020 © All Rights Reserved.
Kayleigh Mickayla Mooney and Kevin Michael Mooney.
For any permissions, including to use or copy, in part or in whole, please contact:
<u>kmmlaw12@gmail.com</u>.
978-0-578-73131-5

Preamble.

I. "...Here in the Continue..."

Sitting on the crystal shores of Ceili Cay with you; brilliant atmosphere presides; I see the whales off in the distance; illuminated glowing jellyfish floating in the sky; shooting stars zipping across the universe; night and day combined in a blush of fragrant scarlet bloom and golden spirit light; the sea and sky blurred into one; turquoise bleeds into purple; the white sand beneath our feet; holding hands across the void; one dimension fused from two; we are eternity; we are love; we are light; we, here in the present; here in the current; here in the continue...then the rains come and blot out this tranquil scene; thick sheets of Diamas Regn; and I am subdued;

"Daddy, try thanking God. As we start this new today, and you weigh the grief journey in the next twenty four hours, remember the gift we live. You think about this all day long each day, the second truth, the counterbalance. So let's start right now in this moment. Turn to God and let's start this day over, Daddy."

Okay, Kakes. You are right, of course. (Breathe).

God, thank you for the opportunity to be with my Daughter today, here sitting on her bed with her, in this miraculous essence. Through the horrible tragedy and transition You elevated Kayleigh to a status of a guardian angel, an angel of the Highest Orders, alive in her higher body of light, in which she has been since that fateful, innocent night of August 17, 2017. As she took her last breath listening to my voice, in my arms and presence lying in the street, our souls locked together as she transitioned right through me in a flash, sitting on my right hand side in her million points of light, inverting our holy relationship and embracing me and speaking to me and flooding me with her angelic presence, as she has done every day since her physical life tragically and so shockingly ended while trying to simply cross a street to come home. That is the miracle. The faith. The hope. You gave her the power of a guardian. And she is sitting on her bed with me right now as she and I write this introduction to this fourth book in the Exuma series; and we are also together on Ceili Cay in Exuma Infinite underneath the bands of Auroral, embracing each other. So, God, thank you for this opportunity to be, today, right now, present and actively engaged with my beautiful Daughter, in whom I am so extremely proud; who I miss physically with every aching cell of my humanity; who I travel with down this road, hand in hand, in glory despite her physical passing.

You smiled.

"God, thank you for the opportunity to be with my Father today. He knows the two truths. He has never misunderstood it. He grieves so heavily, his burden and opportunity so great, watching his beloved Daughter physically pass in his arms, and feeling me just explode through that human barrier as my life, my soul, expanded out of that human condition at fifteen, three months and two days old. In the miracle of my intercession, it was automatic that I would begin immediately trying to test the channels in my new life to direct, guide and bring healing light to my family, one of my main purposes and meanings of my current status of life. And I do. To Daddy. To Mommy. To my little Brother. To all. Thank you, God, for the power of intercession; the power to be in my body of light both in Heaven, our Exuma Infinite, as well as here on earth in my body of light in the physical world. I'm just a sweet, good girl from Cleveland Heights, and, through an untimely and innocent accident, now I have elevated into my truest understanding, into my full being, into a guardian angel, and I am so blessed. Thank You. All glory. All glory…"

II. "...Diamas Regns..."

No matter the gains we have made spiritually, the rains will come. No matter the ground we have covered over these merging two worlds, the rains will come. No matter how present and majestic you are day to day, the rains will come. For I live in this duality - the first truth of the daily suffering of the physical death of one of my children in childhood, and the second truth of her soul transitioning and her life continuing after her physical body died, in essence, the continuation, albeit in a much different vein, of her life, our relationship, and all the glory that results from that union. No matter the magnitude of the second truth, the first truth is also always present, and the rains will come.

They are heavy sheets of grief that come in steady waves, as sure as the ocean has water, as sure as the air has its wind; these are poisonous, dangerous rains at times. Grief at its finest. Ripping, tearing, shredding, gauging. Sheets of dangerous shards of glassy diamonds, like the pummeling storms on Jupiter and Saturn that are a part of their nature, their culture, their daily existence. Now too, these rains are a part of my daily existence in one form or another. There is no hand I can raise to stop the storms. In the fighting, the turbulence just elevates. There is only absorbing, processing each sheet of rain, reconciling each wave upon its arrival. The only way through is through. I walk in the rains when the rains come, sometimes through a beach field of unbearable darkness. I walk, too, in the sunlight of Exuma Infinite when the sky is sparkling brightly in the haze of summer glow. Together, this is now my life, a life balanced enough to breathe; a life worthy in my promise to never dishonor my Daughter and never use my Daughter's innocent accident as an excuse for any failure in my life.

You, Kayleigh, My Love, help me navigate the Diamas Regns; through the centuries and across the dimensions of space and time, through the solar system and beyond this magnificent universe; in the emerald star nurseries and in the sacred space between our eyes, with the bridges of our noses touching and joined playfully. And this with courage, and at times little else, I conquer the moment. I rise with you, to your encouragement, to your delight. I hold your loving hand. I walk in your halo. I breathe of your light. I brace against the force of a hurricane and face the Diamas Regns and emerge...somewhat dry.

AMOR IMMORTALIS

"In a New Configuration"

As accustomed as light is to the sun,
We are accustomed to this very special one,
In her human days,
This child that we've raised,
Look at her with joyous pride,
The expressions on her face,
The smell of her golden hair,
The laughter in her voice ablaze,
Her presence, compassionate and wise,
The ocean cerulean blue breath in her eyes;

We are unaccustomed to her body of light,
Since the tragic angst in that August night,
When her flesh succumbed to what no one could survive,
Since the moment I held her in my arms,
And knowing total safety in my arms,
She physically died;

Like the sun that explodes out over a clear day,
Like the ocean when the water is so transparent,
That each shell below offers vast color,
Each sea-plant sways in dancing current,
Each blazing beam of light flickers in refraction,
Like gem stones sparkling in liquid promise,
Flack, oh fire light, ignite a reef in underwater flame;

In a new configuration,
A golden dream,
A golden reality,
A golden opportunity in a tragic situation,
We grow,
We grow,
We grow…

...In a new chapter, on another stage,
Blessed with intercession,
With the status of a saint,
She has mastered her new essence,
This flesh a million galaxies bright,
As this family of four work itself into,
An elevated station,
A new configuration,
In the continuance of her life...

...Blessed be the believer who shall breathe the living waters,
Of eternal light.

"Harmonizing New Voices"

We were harmonizing our voices within minutes,
Trying out yours as you shifted,
Your vocals hit tones that no human could mimic,
In the new orchestra, your voice lifted,
And carried your Father away,
Blending our light into stronger twining,
A cord that can never be broken,
I listened intently for your voice,
For every breath of yours spoken,
And heard you, my Love,
Within seconds within the wind,
We began harmonizing our voices,
And though there is a veil,
That veil is very thin,
And so we walk as we've always walked,
With new voices,
Into the within.

"Love is Immortal"

The Infinite Endless,
More endless than the universe exposes its stars,
More engaging than the ocean,
That never shows its deepest scars,
Love is immortal,
Love is immortal,
As immortal as we are…

Continuing throughout the perpetual,
The soul's most inalienable light,
Unmistakable,
Unbreakable,
Durable, yet pliable, shatterproof life,
She walks in Exuma,
She walks on this street,
She walks in the air of the water,
In the rash of a thunder heat;

She sits with her Father,
We sit and fulfill our charts,
We press brushstrokes of artful paint blush,
Across each other's hearts,
These cords of living light that cannot be removed,
Indelible, indestructible,
Ineradicable we are,
For we are the truth within the truth,
The sun within the spark,
Fear not, Daddy,
Fear not,
For we know who we are…"

...We are,
Absolute and unassailable,
Ineffaceable, we thrive,
An inviolable gift from God,
That transcends worlds,
The mooring of our lives,
As we walk through these portals,
Into the Infinite Endless,
From shore to shore to shore,
Through door to door to door,
For love is immortal,
Our love is complete,
Yet it expands even further,
Even more...

...In the golden rash of a thunder heat.

"We Are Mycelium"

We are mycelium,
Each one of us it's root,
Intertwined in the cords of love,
And branching out shoot by shoot;

We are a jovial communion related by the heart,
An electric blue netting interwoven of sparks,
And fire channels,
And spiritual veins that expand and spiral,
Across the universe,
Singing in a chorus of overflowing joy,
Verse by lovely verse,
And compassionate words born of wind,
Symbolic language between us groomed,
Like electrochemical conversations,
From womb to womb to womb;

We are one in the cosmic webbing,
Emitting empathy in moments upsetting,
Sending messages through pain receptors,
To alert of danger,
In the siege and surge of weather,
That blasts the soul with life's discord,
We are all mycelium,
In a neural net of sorts.

"She Can Elevate Into Her Angelic Status As She Wishes"

Just beyond our sight,
Yet clearly in our presence,
Just beyond the human eye,
In her brilliance and essence;

I want to be blinded by your beauty,
It would be worth the shattering of lens,
I want to see you in your elevation,
Where your soul into God's light blends,
I would be willing to lose my eyesight,
If the light for one moment I could comprehend,
For I ache for the physical presence of my Daughter,
Though I feel you each day...

...End to end.

"Dissolve the Dimensions"

In the crux of an enduring presence,
In the realm of truth and higher essence,
Behold the spectacle of a family in drastic change,
Dissolving the dimensions,
Merging the planes,
No separate sections,
And not just re-arranged,
She is clearly diverting two rivers,
To flow into one wave,
That travels within the light of living water,
Together, current, present, engaged.

"Rabboni*"

Sacredly, this, analogously,
And mentioned only in humble breath,
For the journey is symbolic,
In each physical death;

Mary, in that moment,
Was the church on this earth,
The only witness thus far in that moment,
To hear His resurrected word;

And I, though no claim to anything,
Felt a similar flash of brilliance in sight,
When my Daughter transitioned,
And I felt her in her Higher Life;

The promise of the spirit,
The fulfillment of the soul,
"Rabboni," she uttered gently, simply,
When He approached her on that road;

And so, for it seems a likewise parable,
That He would wish his angels to sing,
Rabboni, my God, in the paramount,
Rabboni, as well, my Daughter...

...For the teachings that you bring.

The Aramaic word "Rabboni" means "My Teacher."

"There Are Miracles We Miss"

We cannot see every grain of light in hand,
Like envisioning a whisper,
Though strain we may to see,
A vapor trail,
A doorway through the holy veil;

We cannot leave this static plain completely,
To capture visions painted by the visionary,
For she is celestial,
And she and I…

…We are not of this world,
Yet I am still encased in human vessel,
And you are both a guardian angel,
As well as my little girl…

…And so it is with focus I strive and strain to see,
Every single grain of light you offer to me,
Still, there are miracles we miss just before our faces,
Miracles that our eyes cannot translate,
When we hesitate…

…Looking through whispers to see the silhouette...

…Of our Daughter's face.

"The Epic Journey of Twenty Four Hours"

Today is a day now like any other day,
In a skiff upon the water,
With rotted boards and starboard listing,
In the backwash of trauma and tragedy,
And the heartache,
And all that I am missing;

This daunting and complex equation,
This life is so hard,
No matter the situation,
In full color and in our faces,
Surviving the physical death of my child,
My life is as hard as a life can get,
Living in the wake of this trauma,
Having to face another day,
"A twenty hour slice of destiny," as Fish would say...

...Yet nothing is quite like this,
To be so wounded and forced at the helm,
Such a delicate balance not to get overwhelmed,
And I do,
And when I do,
I come back to the great fact in your grace...

...Always present before physical death,
You are now more present than you have ever been...

...And into your open hands I fall.

"A Hurricane on a Wooden Skiff"

(i) Cradled in an Antique Hull

A sturdy boat for the ages,
Plates of thick paint chips like leather skin,
It rolls on the ocean,
And moves with the howling wind,
Powered by sweat and resolve,
And a veil of Heaven promised thin,
He pounds through the rising waves,
As the water explodes around him,
And deep into the valley,
And high into each next crest,
He jags the boat with the antique hull,
That climbs the tempest,
At his behest;

(ii) Daughter Lighthouse

There is a light that is brighter,
Than the world can be dark,
She sets herself upon Exuma hill,
And like a lighthouse with a brilliant spark,
She flashes her beacon,
That cuts through a hurricane's heart,
She draws on a cord of eternal love,
That prevents them from being apart,
She calls though the window,
Like a spiraling shooting star,
That catches her Father's eye,
And draws him towards her arms;

(iii) The Madness of Grief

And the sea cascades with violence,
On an apocalyptic stage,
And the winds reach two hundred miles per hour,
That lift the waters from the ocean's face,
And the sounds of deafening blindness,
Conspire for him a salty cage,
Yet with his hand upon his heart,
He bursts through the walls of this madness,
With unbridled faith;

(iv) Arrival on a Wooden Skiff

He rides a hurricane on a wooden skiff,
Nothing more provided him,
Nothing less to give,
As westward clouds keep spinning away,
And the calmness comes to this,
The ocean settles into rolling waves,
Collapsed with bloody fingers,
And blistered, curled tight fists,
He shakes from the exhaustion,
As the smoke from waters lifts,
The aqua turquoise color emerges,
As the sun presents its gifts,
And he floats on into the shallows,
And finds his Daughter pacing,
With heart awake and racing,
Waiting,
Waiting...

...For him.

"A Guardian Angel's Hands"

She places her golden palm on the crown of my head,
She opens the window to the soul,
When the panes are condemned,
She breathes across the eyes where the hope seed is spread,
And proves beyond doubt a life without end.

"Sitting on the Front Steps Under the Stars"

I sit on the front steps under midnight guardian stars,
Waiting for your return from down the street, every night,
With the trees singing psalms to me,
As today's weight gifts slumber eyes,
And the closing of conscious day comes,
In its generous yet furious retreat;

Yet in the space to my right side,
Where the wind changes inflection,
As you grace a channel to communicate,
And my shoulder senses your affection,
I hear your sweet and lovely voice,
Chanting my name,
Enchanting the sound,
Enchanted, though mortally pained,
I scream out loud,
I scream out to the dispassionate, quiet, motionless stars...

...Though few know this hardship,
And fewer own this road,
We are the ones we've been waiting for,
Wrote a Hopi elder,
That found the parchment of our souls,
And left its mark and its creed,
To defend in all that are,
Praising the sky,
And watching the stars,
Prompting those stars,
Light up this endlessness,
Of all that we have lost,
That range my mournful eyes...

...And all that we have gained,
For the soul, it never dies...

...Through an accident your physical body taken,
It leaves me sitting here on the steps nightly,
Gazing down the street,
Forsaken,
Awaiting to see you step up the sidewalk,
While you hold my hand,
And wrap your arm around my heartbeat...

...My Angel,
My Daughter,
My child.

"Her Sunrise That Burns Through the Gaps"

And in the moment when the grief comes to overwhelm,
When my soul nearly succumbs,
To a sadness like no other,
When the Diamas Regns come,
To batter me with tiny shiny objects,
In sheets of sharp jewels that, by the millions,
Zip by my ears in an aggressive collective hum,
Of spiritual intimidation,
I raise my eyes through the diamond storms,
And through the emotional radiation,
And scream out against the odds,
To secure my child's hand...

...And suddenly the rains collapse,
And the storms lapse,
I sense her presence,
Immediacy,
In the sunrise that burns through the gaps...

...There is a power that explodes in sacred yellow bands of light,
That swirl through a soothing blue haze,
That washes through the sky,
As she flashes the corners of my eyes in white sparkles,
The signs of Heaven revealed,
Yet we do not need figures in the sky,
To know that Heaven is real,
For it comes in those moments,
Touched by miracles,
And in the way that we feel,
Beyond visual proof,
We know when it is just the wind,
And when it is you...

..."Daddy, you know our truth,
Mommy, my brother and you are my home,
And I am so in love with you,
I will never let you do this alone..."

...My Daughter, an accident stole the physical from your life,
Yet altered only your body from flesh to light,
And in the continuance,
As your soul enhanced and continued,
Your brilliance shines so bright,
That no storming Diamas Regn,
Can ever block your Father from you.

"Ultraviolet Hands"

Again and again,
I lay my hands on the crown of your head,
I lay my hands where your third eye is spread,
I lay my hands on your heart,
When your heartbeat sours and ebbs,
I lay my hands on your tongue,
When words from the soul should be said,
I lay my hands on your ears,
To open the channels condemned,
I lay my hands on your soul itself,
Into which the book of my soul...

...Is penned.

"Thorne Beach Access"

When these daydreams may remind you,
I've been stopped many times by this thief,
Hold my soul for ransom,
At the end of the barrel of grief;

Few of the ages have suffered,
The suffering done unto me,
Caught in an accident, Kayleigh,
How on earth, God, could this be?

Child, dance on the sand by the sea,
Walking hand in hand with me,
Will you find living creatures by the water,
And return them to breathe;

Child, before you could walk on your own,
I carried you in my arms as a baby,
And every year until fifteen,
We walked and talked and shared this dream,
Shark fishing together here,
Under Jekyll midnights and summer steam;

Now the nightmares are as sure as the sunset,
Sometimes they break many times in the day,
They stop me from breathing,
Wave after wave after waterless wave;

There is a thin line that I'm holding,
I don't know how much more I can take,
After my Daughter was ripped from my arms,
Thorne Beach with never be the same;

I see now only my footprints, impressions,
As I walk this sandy face,
Though I know you are here, my Love,
Like waves of wind are fleeting,
So too, can flee this faith…

…So suddenly…

…The thunder on a distant earth catch my ear,
Turn my head,
The Regns in the duality,
In the backdrop of Thorne Beach,
In a solemn darkness shed.

"Jekyll Exuma"

Where the sky meets the ocean,
Where the sea and cloud meet,
She is standing on horizons...

...Waiting for me;

In the images of turquoise,
On Bahamian sandy fleece,
And another scene of white sand,
On a Georgia stretch of beach;

They blend in the merging,
Brown waters and aqua green,
A wild jungle barrier island,
And a Caribbean isle of steam;

These are her heavens,
That have held her feet,
One in her vibrant physical days,
And one now in her Higher Peace;

And the sky meets the ocean,
Where the angels are gathering,
As I ebb and flow in growth and grief,
She can hardly contain her joy...

...Waiting for me.

"Checking the Turtle Nests"

Under the blaze of the spirals of the Milky Way,
In the deep of the darkness of night,
Like an angelic fairy,
Making her way down the beach,
Splashing golden glitter dust in her wake,
It spreads, sparkling in the wind and the breeze,
She is bouncing dune to dune,
Peeping through sea oat,
Checking the turtle nests,
And blessings, these nests with hope,
Under a summer moon…

…And the hours are miles,
And the miles find her Father in heartbreak fluctuation,
Ranging the Loggerhead nesting grounds,
A Daddy and Daughter,
In this new configuration,
Now in different body types,
(One glancing down the beach would see just one figure),
A grieving Father in this sorrowful situation,
With a hole in his soul,
(But what the other may not know),
He is not alone,
He is walking with his beautiful Daughter,
Elevated into a guardian angel,
This Second Truth is his salvation,
That raises a smile on his face,
Doing what these tow have always done,
Laughing, talking, and walking through each trauma,
With each step she counsel's him to take.

"Father Daughter Nightly Sea"

Bathing in the moonlight under a canopy of stars,
The wounds they sting in the platinum scars,
The metal drains from me, distantly succumbed,
The ocean waves that slap my body like a drum,
All my days from that moment until now,
All my days I've had to learn to live somehow...

...How...

...The sash of the tails of the Milky Way blaze,
Spin, though my eyes cannot seem to see that spiral display,
So it comes to this in the cruel crucible of fate,
To feel you here is just a matter of deep faith,
All my love I give to you, my child,
Under the seascape,
And the silver moonscape,
I see your beautiful face,
Your presence right here next to me,
Listening to your voice in the winds,
And the waves and the wilds...

...On this beach of our nightly sea.

"Scarlet Purple Whales"

We face this tragedy and this miracle each day with unbridled courage; a family tested beyond the range of the acceptable, beyond the comprehension of all, except for those few who have likewise suffered such devastation and physical death of a child in childhood;

We see the worst and the best; the deepest suffering and the highest rejoicing; for our Daughter was physically killed in an innocent accident at fifteen years, three months and two days old; and, our Daughter transitioned into her current, active, present life in her spiritually body of light, miraculously sitting beside us and engaging her family just as she always has, yet now much more powerfully in her elevated self;

These are the festive grounds of scarlet purple whales, swimming through the vortex of space and time, of sea and sky, of life and Higher Life; these are the gentle souls, the mighty souls, that sing to their children, that sing to their parents; that range the glory of eternal rainbow nebula seas as a family blessed in compassionate presence, of immortal love, of endless anamchara.

"Kayleigh Sea"

Opening the window of the sea,
The ocean a doorway it becomes,
A portal to another world,
Anchored by our souls that glow of moon and sun,
In the window where the scented breeze flows,
And swirls into liquid gold,
You were swimming there,
Swimming there with me,
If only I could remain every second of every day,
Adrift in Kayleigh Sea.

"The Loggerheads and the Sea Sky"

Loggerheads, like celestial birds,
Swim through space on gliding flippers,
Crossing through the horn of Orion,
And feasting at the edge of the Big Dipper,
Graced by angel candlelight,
She lights a golden road through the sea sky,
Calling the Loggerheads, each one by special name,
To swim up beside her,
And settle in her radiant, outstretched arms.

"Seagulls on the Morning Glide"

Seagulls flocked in rainbows emerge from morning smoke,
Spread out across the beachfront with wings as white as snow,
Sun that catches feathers, reflects the light of hope,
That glistens on their bodies,
That glistens in their souls.

"An Ocean Of Wind"

An ocean of wind,
Its water nothing more than veils of breeze,
That wave like liquid,
In a tapestry that dances just under closed eyelids,
Where the dimensions dissolve,
Where the tension gives,
And all is resolved,
Where the higher self lives,
Deep within the currents and the tidal pull,
Of a deep and vibrant ocean of wind.

"Sitting in the Ocean"

Breathe turquoise air,
Deeply in the aura,
Deeply in the aqua green,
Breathe the liquid flora,
That flows within me...

...I spend my days just thinking of you,
All day long,
Grieving you,
Breathing you,
Needing you,
Seething for you,
Seeing you in my memories,
In my dreams,
In the corner of my eyes,
In the present in the halo seams,
All across the beachfront where we come together,
When we meditate,
Where we do not hesitate,
In a passionate, compassionate love,
All day,
I spend all day just being with you...

"Circles and Circles"

Circles within circles within circles,
Interlacing diamonded wreaths,
An organic growth of the spirit,
When nurtured with belief,
We gather these gems after the rains,
By the millions left strewn on the beach,
A voice for the light in each jewel,
A rainbow sparkle one for each,
That engages life with its fuel,
Each raindrop, pure, unique,
They pepper the atmosphere with sparkles,
When they fall in heavy sheets,
Like blessings that dance all around us,
And glisten at our feet,
We task our hands in the gathering,
And weave these sacred wreaths,
That we build with each new rainfall,
And stronger when interweaved,
We love and hold each other,
And into each we breathe.

"Life Elevated (On This Path)"

"Daddy, trust God, trust me and trust this path; it is the only path upon which light finds us both; let's keep walking, hand in hand, even when you can't quite feel my hand, Daddy, in the eternity of now. It is so beautiful, Daddy, if you could see it from my vantage point; if you could see it from my eyes; like you would when I was a little girl, lying on the floor or the grass or the beach sand with me and trying to see from the angle at which my eyes viewed the world. Like that, Daddy.

When the rains come, and they come daily, grab my hand and try to see the bigger worlds from my eyes. I know, Daddy, and I'm so sorry. It was such an innocent, simple and perfect accident. You love me so much. I am so honored by that love. I always have been. My untimely physical death does not change that; it only elevates it.

I sense a storm approaching you, Daddy. Smell it in the air. You feel it in your stomach, your chest, your heart. We can do this, Daddy, together. I love you."

"Ambient Grief"

Sometimes life is ambient noise,
And I cannot hear its voice,
Sometimes the ragged white noise,
Is the settling rhythm…

…Of choice…

…Ask me in a moment,
The world may shift again,
Though trapped on this equatorial band,
The world may lift and bend,
Though steady are the sorrows,
It will mix, collapse and descend,
And again ascend,
For the poles through which I journey know,
A man who grieves for his child,
Grieves a thousand fold.

"Whale Whispers"

Sometimes life is ambient noise and I cannot hear,
Not beyond the heart where the sound waves disappear,
I lapse,
I cry,
I laugh in the powerlessness,
That has imprisoned my eyes;

Then, a sound, it glances up over the sadness,
Their angelic songs echo off of cloud banks,
Hug the sea,
Whispers of the mighty ones,
That explore the outer edges,
Of the water of eternity,
They never spend a moment,
Without the intentions of empathy,
They never waiver in fidelity,
The love for family, their bloodstream,
They call to me in chorus,
They call to me, believe,
They call to me while riding the waves,
In a sacred melody.

"Raining Diamas"

The pink rings that halo the planet,
Saturn cloaked in an ethereal hold,
A temperance of a Caribbean coastline,
Beneath the gaseous atmosphere unfolds,
Stretching out into gardens,
Like the ones that only sprout from gold,
She sees the grottos and the tiny rivers,
Over which these rainbows flow;

Sheets of jeweled teardrops shred the atmosphere,
Like storms of shards of glass that rage with squalls of fear,
And here, once again, the rains have come,
The rains have come...

...Where the pastel rings smolder,
And the smoke from antiquity gardens steam,
Were it not for the fact that we are older,
Than the lives that we have seen,
I would not be found within this breath,
That takes me to the next,
And the next,
And the next...

...As sheets of jeweled teardrops explode in opal jade,
And scratch across the eyes the valleys they have made,
So beautiful the artistry when viewed from outer space,
Yet not when one is caught in the rains,
And subject to its rage...

...And although your life, your presence is undeniable,
Your closeness close at hand,
The rains still come pounding daily in the duality,
Dissolving the will of man...

"The Bones of Thunder"

Have you ever heard one thousand echoes,
Trapped in the empty chamber of an echo,
Compiling in the vibrating tundra,
Steal walls compounding the shrill,
With no audible breaks;

This storm, it screams across the sky's frontier,
Searching desperately for its tone,
Severing the air, ripping it asunder,
Bone by bone by brittle bone...

...Until the lightning comes,
And it comes,
And it comes...

...And makes an audience of our home,
In the quell of a conscience,
Compelled to run aground,
Nonstop thunder for hours on end,
With reverberating sounds,
Rattles the engine,
And it, with mighty hand,
Flattens the voice in the maelstrom...

...We are nonetheless.

"Fire Spears"

Earth shake, a flash, a straggler comes,
With a vengeance,
In the heat of a humid rash,
On an opal night,
Burning the miles from the cloud valleys,
In an instant,
Exploding into the caverns in the back of the eyes,
We did not see this coming,
And now it is here,
Simmering beneath my feet,
As I toll the blindness,
In a thundering companion,
This spear of fire light,
That has pierced my heart,
That has come to electrify my life...

...If I can survive the strike.

"Three Feet Deep In A Quagmire Jolting"

Eyes open yet three feet underneath mud,
There is not much to see down here,
Where all sense of direction disappears,
In a cauldron I'd soon rather sympathize,
Than stretch out in the bubbling ooze,
Like slugs that cup to these eyes,
That leave a slimy bruise,
This quagmire here is jilting,
A quicksand that slowly digests me,
And vomits as it consumes,
Me...

...When one minute into this suffering,
Feels like a century of pain,
When the life becomes a challenge too difficult to bare,
Yet there is no other way,
Three feet deep in a quagmire jolting,
Grief, we meet again,
We meet again,
We meet again...

Hurricane huddled hibernating in my head,
Like a tightly taut barbed wire across the heart is twisted,
Spread,
In a tantalizing web,
In a traumatic affect,
And just as the quagmire conquers my breath,
The angels that support me come flooding,
Like an ocean finds a lower frontier,
Like waves of liquid light that swirl about,
in an ubiquitous atmosphere,
They enter the mud zone with me,
And try to pull me out of here.

"Plateaus, Paradigms and Paradoxes"

Rather I would on a miracle or on a polar opposite pain,
Yet in this moment, which I can't explain,
I trudge the wetland hinterland,
In the morass of swampy forests and lost on lunar plains,
Plateaus and paradigms,
Parade of paradoxes, stagnant frames,
They break for fodder temporarily and then,
Plot their course upon the trail again,
Laughing in circles,
Contemptuously circling the drain...

...In the normal settings of human challenges,
These would straighten themselves out,
But not in cases so sacred as this,
Not with the physical death of a child,
No, there are no workarounds,
There is only the grief that can drive one insane;

A beautiful woman – an angel - a little girl,
Wrapped up into one individual,
In a certain moment in time,
Just before the devastation,
Just before the shifting on the celestial poles,
I have snapshots of her face at fifteen,
A vibrancy like none other I have known,
I hold on for dear life when the plateaus come for me...

...Knowing the cartography of my soul;

Like bins filled with her childhood art,
(As a child she painted daily),
With titles such as, "Kitty Mermaid Mom and Daughter,"
And "My Daddy Moon" and "Mommy Night,"

Where pink and purple petals,
Picked from flowers that bloom in space,
Rooted into the air itself,
Of which the charms of life has chased,
Across indigo star fields,
That blossom like her voice echoes in these sacred pieces,
Her brushstrokes of her life once ignited,
Found a myriad of releases;

Now she pulls these images from the depths of living water,
And, while in the span of visitation,
Places these fragrances and flavors in her Mother's heart,
Places these forward momentums in her Father's feet,
Staggering through the paradigms and the plateaus,
Shot through with a thousand indignities,
And a million misunderstood arrows,
That mark the road with the rich life's blood…

…Of my wounded soul.

"Walking in a Fog Bank"

It is like a midday bank of fog so thick,
That the sun is obscured in the haze,
Though the curtains collect in these grieving eyes,
The sun is still high in the sky ablaze,
(I just cannot see the light),
While the stomach lay quarantined and sick,
Beyond the shadows of despondency,
Beyond the veils of fear,
While I troll in the smoky webs of this mirage,
I cannot feel you...

...A feeling to which no emptiness can be compared,
Though you are beside me,
Literally...right here.

"This Life"

Overwhelmed, I want to throw up this wretched life,
That nauseates me in its cruelty and inequity,
That my child could suffer an innocent accident,
That thieved her of her physical life,
And destroyed us in the severing...

...We are raw courage the likes the world can rarely hold,
But there are times when I am asked to walk with no feet,
With no lungs,
Upon this harsh and painful road...

Kayleigh, My Daughter, My Love,
I scream out to you,
In opal blue, in aqua blue, in turquoise bruise,
And collapse in your arms,
Sit here in a delicate silence with me,
Whisper God's secrets,
Whisper God's dreams,
Whisper God's vision,
That redirects this scene,
Show me the miracle,
Show me the light,
Show me the way forward,
Through this excruciating life;

Scream out the answers,
In your Fenian warrior's scream,
Show me through the labyrinth,
Leaving bread crumbs at my feet,
Scream joyful encouragement,
So deep in this grief,
So steep in this fight,
Show me the way forward,
Through this excruciating life.

"The Scar Cage"

Time is no friend,
Time stretches scars across the skin of life,
With expansive sorrows,
From the initial impact seed of trauma,
Rippling through and damaging tomorrows,
The scar obfuscates and alters,
As the triumphs come as do the falters,
Though we know exactly who we are,
Change stretches the scar cage,
Change wretches us with rage,
Change comes with the thief of time,
Whose gift is not erasure...

...But the elongation of the scar.

STORMS OF THUNDER DIAMONDS

"Every Morning...Into the Fight"

Through the darkest mirages of night,
Through the exhaustion and into the fight,
Armed to the teeth with the light of my soul,
Armed with the faith that we dearly hold,
Every morning,
Into the struggle I go,
Into the struggle I go...

"In an Opal Cradle"

Royal purple, opal splash,
A vibrant dark lavender rash,
Blending in a whitish, bluish, green,
Swirling in the stomach of thunder,
Gurgling in the cumulonimbus spleen,
Filtering the sky blood in its vapor screen,
As hungry as a hurricane for walls of wind to make,
Where the cloud fields rumble furiously,
And reverberate as the ground shakes,
With a resonance of bewilderment,
Of the coming of a violent storm,
While the royal purple maelstrom,
In an opal cradle forms.

"Storms of Sprites of Thunder"

Hush, quilted miles of air above towering artworks of cloud,
Thunderstorms shake beneath their whitish bloated shrouds,
Flickering scarlet pixies dancing in the moonlit shadows,
Sprites that range the black-green, tourmaline night sky,
Electric shapes spike these cumulonimbus beasts,
Deep out in the ocean in the east,
Luminous reddish orange flashes charge,
In clusters, blush and rash,
Into the heart they dash,
Impaling clouds with thunder scars...

...That leave no man his eyes.

"Sheets of Diamond Rains"

Bliss, in this halo, a beautiful day, rise,
Rainbow vibrant color explode across their faces,
Ultraviolet haze ripples with holy steam,
That elevates in these sacred spaces,
Where we stand shoulder to shoulder,
Where we sing and laugh and share jumping embraces…

…In the heat of summertime,
In the humid blaze of a July Cleveland night,
"The world in green and blue,"
Bono sang,
In that time when everything in my life was bright,
As bright as the halo that graced this beautiful day,
As bright as the smile on your face,
"Now, that's a beautiful day!"

Then came…

…Those shards and sheets of diamond rains.

"Thunderhead"

Giant convective towers,
Fleshed of moist air and billowing thunderhead,
Meshing together with deep vapor clouds,
And arid air and humid salty webs,
These category five hurricanes erupt in my head,
Rip the skin from the earth in the spinning,
In the human shedding,
In the deep august shred;

Markers of convection,
The lightning tracks across magical domains,
Turbulence, pulling heat, mixing together,
A Frankenstein of invariable weather,
The visible cloud peeks topple,
And drive downward in an avalanche of diamonds,
Rain that poisons the grottos lined with flowers,
And cover the gate posts with jagged firefly dust;

In the rash of a thunder heat,
Lightning like a heartbeat explodes,
Ripping at the celestial sanctuaries,
Ripping out the well tracked stone of Jupiter's roads,
The convection is a folly,
Ask poor Saturn in its turn,
For both planets bear the scars of beauty,
And the depths of the Diamas burn.

"Cement Lungs"

The liquid stone hardens,
Another vein has been sprung,
In the cracks and the crevasses,
Filling in the lungs,
With no space to falter,
And nor the light to breathe,
The cement coagulates,
And bubbles and seethes...

...And the cruelty comes with an olive branch,
Twisted into a shank,
If it could slam its stalk through my throat,
Into my neck bury its fangs,
As if I could fight off the torture,
As if I could pass these stones of pain,
My dearly beloved Daughter,
I will reach through the hardened mesh...

...With the last of my strength,
At any lengths,
I will breathe, though cement has webbed the lungs,
I will breathe into each grievous vein...

...Until the strain has shifted...

...When...

"Pluvial Crystalline Carbon"

The grief, marked by a period of increased rainfall,
Left its scratches on the soul,
Where a million stones battered the light,
Like diamond hale that slammed into fragile fields of emotion,
Exploding upon contact with the human soil,
And spreading tinier fragments,
That filled the crevasses and the cracks,
An entire landscape, strewn with shards and jagged objects,
Like stinging glass,
Where an effortless river bed once toiled,
Scraping the entire earthen body,
With the scars so deeply etched into this one...

...A Father who has seen too much.

"Opal Smoky Fields"

And enter, thrown through these perilous gates,
Grief, the venom that conflates the flame in the veins,
Suffocating in the aftertaste,
Of this situation that I am forced to consume,
Could there be a worse fate,
Not in this world nor in its darkest gloom;

My flesh, the kindling the thirsty bonfire ate,
Ravaging across this desolate, arid landscape,
Where the ghost crabs scurry deep underground,
Where the seagulls on a trade-wind escape,
And no life nor any signs of life are found,
Under opal smoky fields…

…The world stood still and gasped in a collective breath,
A city wailed as its innocence was exiled,
Shocked by the most unlikely of physical deaths,
A child!
A precious child!
A perfectly vibrant child!
A perfectly healthy child!
A brilliant child!
A beautiful child!
This child, lying in the street at my feet…

…My child…!

"The Diamond Harvest"

...In the beginning,
His love wrapped in open palm,
The winds of nature shape the planets,
With atmospheric psalms,
Breathe for the prophet,
The poets and their songs,
For the miracles take many faiths and shapes,
Yet they all seem to belong;

Alleys of space weather,
Great collisions of storms,
In the upper atmosphere,
Where the thunder is born,
The sea of lightning blazes,
In a metamorphic score,
Seed the methane melody,
And soot that hardens to the core,
Squeezing carbon into sparkling diamonds,
That zip through the wind,
Like horrible little daggers,
Like a bullet blows a horn,
And crashes into Saturn,
Where the fields of fire succumb to the scythe,
Of Saturn's intense atmospheric pressure;

Sparkling pillars, fire ice jewels, suspended in the air,
Plate-shaped ice crystals in weather, frigid cold,
Reflecting light downward,
As beams of light descend from the sky,
In the smoke of elongated sparking halos,
That burst in the mid-ground,
Halfway between the eyes and the Source of all light.

"Regn"

If in an avalanche of humid rash,
As the carbon arranged into crystal graph,
In all directions on a precious tear,
That blanket Saturn's horizons,
With storming atmospheres;

I see the front as it approaches,
With its painful reproaches,
And all that will come to bare in just moments away,
When the grief and its argument broaches,
The massive subject of internal hurricanes…

…Shelter not from Regn,
For no shelter long will this sustain,
And shelter, nor from the tyranny,
Of the soul as it, soaked to the bone with pain,
Reaches up through the atrocities,
Of the most unimaginable rains…

…And in the torrent I surmise,
Across the centuries of many, many lives,
We have conquered every year,
We have lived eternally within every tear,
That brings with it the promise of morning lighting,
That shines in the aftermath of showers so brightly,
So brilliantly the flood we share,
Passing hurricanes,
Through the veins…

…Here come,
Here come,
Here come the healing Regns……

"Always Barefoot and in the Dirt"

My perfect little companion,
You were always laughing with your hands digging in the dirt,
You were always smitten with acorns and stones in your hands,
You were always smiling with an artistic eye,
Changing the world any way you can...

...And you dream now into action all that can be,
And alight the blind edges of our eyes so we can truly see,
That you are now higher, my Little Love,
With your fingers in the soils of Saturn,
With your barefoot quenched in Exuma tides,
Blowing on the halo of the moon to increase its glow,
Collecting prayers and glittering blessings,
And placing them,
Like tenderly wrapped Christmas presents,
In the center of our souls.

"In the Now and Hand in Hand"

Actually, not only does the theory miss the point, but there is no need to "wait" for the "again" when it, our togetherness, is happening right now; when it, our relationship, is continuous without a break; when it, our love and presence with the other, is a line unbroken between us, that no physical death can alter. So I do not need to wait until we "meet again," for I meet you here where I always meet you - in the seat of our souls, one beside the other, courageously walking our current lives in a continuum of eternity; in an unbreakable commitment of love and light.

Though we currently occupy different body types, mine in human flesh and yours in a spiritual body incarnate of a million points of light, we have only been partially "parted" by your physical body's death, but not by your true, higher body, which sustains life after exiting your beautiful, physical form; and the partial parting, that one may assume would be a weakening, is itself a strengthening of your life, and therefore, a potential strengthening of our relationship should I work through the perpetual heartache and learn your new presence and embrace our current road; therefore, as I do, and as you do also, in perfect fidelity to our bond, our spirits walk authentically in the now, hand in hand.

If we can face down and walk through and find the gift and the glory of our immaculate relationship in our current situation, while facing the grief and the sorrow and the sadness that we feel each day; if we can build our relationships with each other in this effortless family of four; if we can, very thoughtfully, find our path through these struggles without distracted struggling, especially when embracing our favorite girl in the worlds, then there is nothing in this world we, this family, and it's individual parts, can't do. That is life on the light in which we endure.

You are the tip of the spear for this family, Babygirl. Keep our feet faithful to the road.

"Super Fluidity"

Incoherent, blindness, us all,
No ceiling, nor flooring, no walls,
Consciousness elevated beyond the material boundaries,
When we let go,
We rise in the never fall;

There is no death,
Flowing without friction,
Flowing without viscosity,
Flowing without fiction,
Flowing without velocity,
Flowing as does the soul,
When it flows without from its Source,
Flowing as this soul does,
On an angelic course;

Is it not man's attribute to theorize and examine,
Is it not man's limit where the mind may cage the soul,
In the halls of disappointment,
In the basement of pointless distress,
In the bandages and triage ointment,
Once used, discarded in a congested corner,
Failing in containment to the drain of a seeping mortal wound,
In the haunts of emotional trauma,
Fifty suns voided and absent of supportive moons,
That hedge our auras in the clip of meteor showers,
In the dreams of crystalline order,
Shall I, like gem stone,
Share the template of the dispossessed,
Who know not the road they could journey,
Like the road that we have braved,
On this unique road through the seas of Heaven,
And Earth,
And the galaxies beyond the grave;

Death?
There is no death,
A superficial construct,
In hinges on the self-centered ethos,
Of human conscience and human conduct,
Where this concept of finality is miscalculated,
And, seeking in the wrong direction,
A mourner may speak with little spiritual inspection,
Or instruction,
As if their loved one who has "passed,"
In in the past,
No,
No,
So far from the truth…

…For there are angels standing beside you,
For we are the light of living water,
Proven by my Daughter,
So let it be…

…So let it be.

"When Sheathed in Human Skins"

…We know,
Many are the obstacles that lurk upon this grievous road,
When sheathed in human skin,
Where the experience is, although not impossible, very thin,
Where the human tendencies constantly expose,
A weakness in this limited capsule,
While my Love, she, graced in effortless body of soul,
Illuminates a thousand fold,
Elevated a million fold,
And smiles upon her Father,
And teaches him all lessons between the earthen poles,
And beyond its solar hold;

Though I, with opal crafted prayers,
Lift my spirit as if jumping up cloud planked stairs,
Ugly are the dangers lurking in my fears,
Ugly are the moments I miss when I miss the now and here,
And so I come back into the human hold,
Aging, in seconds, another century old,
And root my feet like twisted trunks of ancient forests,
And into the deep I go…

"The Groan of the Lantern"

A groan of the lantern,
A pitch of the dark,
He turned around in the blackness,
Like a blinded, wingless, flightless lark,
Empty of song,
Not even a painful bark,
He resumed his pitiless hobbling,
Or upon an outbound track, embark...

...Will he...

...Lost in the wild hinterland strewn of tall trees of sorrow,
And the darkness of feeling alone,
(Though never truly is he on his own);

Sometimes in the throw of the shadow lightning,
With the lantern's voice exposed,
A spirit rise, and lift in the eyes,
Brings new strength to straggling feet;

And his faith built from courage,
Place here each stone by bloody stone,
Bare the rock path to travel through heartache,
Intending firm flesh for this hard road,
Was the clay formed from heartbreak,
Reinforced with spirit bone,
Or did the hope, once thought forlorn,
Show itself in the lantern's groan,
Illuminating the dips and disguises,
Of a labyrinth of entanglement...

...So far from all they have ever known,
He builds from tangle branch,
A boat, his soul, behold.

"Ash Black Purple Rage"

Have you ever had your backbone ripped out from the front,
Your compass smashed,
Yet no quarry of the hunt,
Just a random act of blindness,
The world, what were you thinking of,
When this tragedy struck?

For we are a good family who did everything right,
Yet heartache burned our doorway down,
And set our souls in sorrowful, cunning spiral flight;

Ash black purple rage,
It expounds from these lungs,
Screaming at the universe,
Railing at the heavens,
But she was so young,
So very young..,
My God, my Child was so health and so very young…

And as I was plucked from my life,
And deposited on another planet,
And as my child was ripped from my arms,
In ways I will never understand it,
A rage, a slow burn, percolated,
A rage, for no karma's escapade,
For horrible things can happen,
To the most wonderful of us,
And this, the unthinkable, has happened,
To the very best of us,
This pitiless, passionless perverted world,
In needs people like you,
Kayleigh,
It desperately needs people like you,
And now…

…My Love, I ache with every ounce of my being for you,
As the fires I torched to the Earth's arid skin spread,
Rise, the bonfire of love set by a Father,
Marking our last stand upon this sphere,
Let the flames rise,
Let the smokes race across the distant skies,
And take us away from here...

…Exuma, across the great divide, calls us home.

"Amor Vincit Omnia"

Baby, she has not yet opened up her eyes,
Yet she follows his voice to the heart,
Wrapped in the first few minutes of life,
Or within the continuum, if you'd like,
Of an infinite light…

…Cuddled up in this familiar atmosphere,
In this spectacular encounter with open ears,
Listening to her Father and Mother,
(And several years later, a Brother),
She sailed off from the pristine shores of Exuma,
And into human life,
Where love,
Love,
Love,
Conquers all…

My baby, she could not open her eyes,
Yet she followed my words toward her heart,
Wrapped in those last few moments of life,
Or within this continuum, if you'd like,
Of an infinite light…

…Huddled up in this space that knows no fear,
In this sacred moment of physical death,
With open soul and open heart and open ears,
Listening to her Father as he cradled her,
Just after the accident, and after the fall,
She sailed off towards the pristine shores of Exuma,
And exited human life,
Where love,
Love,
Love,
Conquers all.

"A Galaxy of Sea Turtles"

In loving reverence in you,
Their guardian,
Their guiding light,
Sea turtles gather, as many as there are stars in the sky,
Along this enchanted celestial reef,
Under the rash...

...Of a thunder heat.

"Breathing Colors"

I am again with failing breath and aching flesh,
And painful steps and angry eyes so often rain swept,
Where the keys to the kingdom are hidden,
Is where the grief finds its depth;

Help me climb through the sandy lattice of the wind,
For you never held me tighter than you do now,
And you always bring a bridge with you somehow,
Help me see the light in the day,
Help me cry and scream and process these tears astray,
Help me find courageous step,
Help me daily face the facts of death,
And you always serve to show me how,
That you are here in the here and now;

…As if this human set of eyes came with no instructions,
I banter about in the darkness by the laws of deduction,
A mountain, stone by stone, is its only reduction,
Though a warrior never succumbs,
To such self destructive seduction,
Nor will I ever dishonor you by using your physical death,
For any excuse at failing my life,
In all of the challenges before me yet;

But never could I imagine a tragic accident,
Would slam my soul down and break its knees,
Having to not only grief for my child,
But forced each breath without her physical presence,
And into the wretched chains of duality, I scream,
Please help me see the colors I cannot see,
Please help me breathe the colors all around me,
For I believe,
Touch me in any manner you choose your presence to convey,
I trust you, My Child, with defenseless faith.

"The Garden of the Second Truth"

Through a tempest of natural violence,
And the deeper hurricanes spawned with hurricanes,
Through the last full mile of dedication and devotion,
Through the tribulations of sailing endless oceans,
Through fatigue and diamond rains,
Through the first truth and it's impenetrable pain;

A turquoise ocean garden in the distance,
Just around the next wailing,
Just beyond the next fainting,
On the stalks of knees that are still failing,
A garden with its flora,
And the air ripe for inhaling,
Its scent is the bouquet of love,
Exuma Infinite,
It's light all pervading,
That settles into us,
Just around the next corner...

...That opens to a secret glade,
Tucked into a shoreline that the familial angels,
For us, have made,
Crowned by sacred tidal brush,
Ordained in the sands of time,
That rest under our feet like fluffy pillows,
Sea shell white,
Though just a shade different each grain,
Collected for our troubles,
And blessing our perseverance,
For walking faithfully through the Diamas Regns,
The Second Truth rises through the ashes,
Like the universe has collected every celestial flame,
Illuminating salvation in this harbor,
This harbor that this family has gained.

"Wind Chimes and Ocean Waves"

If the sky and sea and wind and water,
Were tied together by the intuition,
Of my angelic Daughter,
Then you would hear the sounds of the Heavens,
Like a thousand violins alight in her voice;

When the waves curl and crash,
And echo, rumbling in the collapse,
Wind chimes resonate in delicate song,
Water chimes and sand and shells,
And Sand Dollars,
All spin together,
As the coastline gasps,
Like millions of diamonds rattling in and sparked in refraction,
Like an orchestra in crescendo pounds out its final note,
I lift up high and recede deeply below,
I come in and out,
I come and go…

…Praying for turquoise tides,
As high and wide as the skies,
To swallow this pain in an instant of relief,
From insatiable and unsustainable grief,
And a powerlessness like none other can exceed,
My Little Love, my Little Girl,
My Little Baby, my Little World…

…God, when you look into my eyes,
You know its doubt I try to hide,
The question I will not ask shows itself,
But finds no passage in my mouth,
For I resist to ask…

…Why.

"On the Outer Edge of the Out Islands"

(i) Water Art

Where the white sands lift above the water's edges,
Where the turquoise waters line the beach with aqua hedges,
She plays there with the others in the tapestry of souls,
All we have loved and all we choose to hold;

The texture of turquoise shallows,
The bleed of sunrise in its crest and wake,
Water opal prayers confessed on a liquid rosary,
Release against these coral flats as the waves break,
And pulled back into the wild frontier of living water,
We flow…

…Swimming the glittering golden dreams, they gleam,
Like December blue cast in sunlight streams,
Breathing across the breeze,
Effortlessly,
Like stars that bloom and blossom beneath the sea…

(ii) Saturn Oceans

These are the oceans of the soul,
No chart nor compass scales,
These are the oceans of sky, rash of nebula sea,
Where the great migrating whales,
Cross the millenniums with credos of fidelity,
And jellyfish lanterns glow,
And the prophets they proclaim a persistence of faith,
This echo claims my attention,
Your intervention daily,
Though back into a darker fold I go,
For it is the nature of this grief to wound me so;

(iii) Ag

And then, like a breeze, that rattled an empty head,
in an instant into a knowledge void I have regressed,
And without knowledge as the thoughts float on by,
With no concentration the hours might as well be cast aside,
Ag and gnostic,
A net cast so shallow and so wide,
In the churn of the engine,
In the burn of the rub,
In the rash left with lash welt,
In the aftermath of a broken heart's flood;

(iv) The Great Strength in the Diamond Rains

Of tears,
And it is okay, Honey, as I always explained,
As I raised you at my hip,
And flowered your days with an abundance of joy,
And respect, and laughter and love;

I am going to cry on Father's Day,
I am going to cry on Mother's Day,
And I am going to cry on Monday,
And I am going to cry on Thursday,
And I am going to cry at noon and six and eleven,
And the rains will come and the days will curl asunder,
And the horror will storm across my life,
And feel as if the waves have pulled me under,
Where I learn to breathe beneath the water,
Where I learn to grieve and mourn my Daughter,
Each day, and hour, and minute and every faithful second…

"Drizzled in Diamas"

Liquid diamonds consent to the issues embroiling,
Along a peaceful beachfront,
Thought the sky above embroidered in thunder,
Is stirring, and bubbling and boiling,
When the jewels splash into the salty crystal waters,
They melt,
When the spear that caught the heart in its crosshairs,
Left its scar,
Never this wounded before I have felt;

Saturn's sporadic electrical pulses charged the space sea,
That reached its tidal waves to cross the frontier to reach me,
These drizzling nuisance of pitter patter rage,
That thump upon, like nails, a man, a hollow metal cage;

The dimensions sometimes crowd and obscure,
And fall into a trance themselves,
Although I am spending time with her,
I am yet trapped still within my human shell,
And in this frame my yearning is limited by skin,
As I flinch in the subtly of the coming storms,
And screech back into the living hell,
Of not feeling her by my side;

Remaining sensitive to extreme heat,
My immortal memory carries with it a piece of the sea,
Recalled in times of weakness when the soul needs its feet,
Lightning pearls trapped in my dark green eyes,
Expand into the breach,
Reaching out time after time,
No effort remains unheralded,
When the spirit longs to shine.

"Every Second Since"

Too many seconds from that second,
When the world inverted in a catastrophic trauma,
When the world betrayed all sensibility,
When the world murdered tranquility,
In the nursery of a parent's love,
And a young woman's physical life,
As she, in a horrible accident, transitioned,
So many hours ago,
Constructed with tears every second I miss,
I stagger,
I struggle,
I wince,
Every second,
Every second...

...Since.

"Laughing in Diamas Regn"

Every raindrop, in this lightning storm, a well cut diamond,
Singing by the millions in thick sheets of blazing rain,
Radiating bright opal flashes across the fields and the skies,
This liquid light, it sparks as it hits the surface,
Of my face...

...And cleanses wounded eyes...

...You are life, life itself, streaming through my hair,
A pressure zone of love that crashes through a darkened atmosphere,
And awake, I tune these eyes, though closed,
To these angelic waters,
And hear the sweet, soft melody,
Of the verbal conveyance of my Daughter,
Laughing in the rain...

...So clearly, and calling out my name...

...Rejoice, in glory, the showers transcend,
As Heaven and the physical world blend,
And I see this, and I know then,
That there is no after life,
For what comes after...

...That which does not end.

"A Loggerhead Tail"

She is migrating, pulling us along, a magnetic Loggerhead that swims among the celestial rainbows, the star fields, the solar auras; she swims weaving beneath, beside and above the space whales that sing to her compassionately as she passes, knowing this one, this is a sacred one;

The air, the water, once touched and released by her flippers, sparkles in liquid light as a radiant golden tail stretches for miles behind her in her wake; others follow the vibrating light; others bathe in the living water that comes so naturally to her, this sea angel, this guardian of souls;

She is the moon; the tides; the cycles of love eternal; she is a Loggerhead; she is my Daughter, swimming up beside her drowning Father, and lifting my head above the waves with the safety of her frame, my arms draped around her mighty shell; only love resides here. Light is all we know.

"A Wolfe Disk in Which the Dimensions Thrive"

All intermixed,
The universes and dimensions,
Your presence and persistent interventions,
Each elevation,
And ascension,
Each moment of endearing love between us,
Shooting stars that cross the distance of time,
And meet in that perfect gaze in the sacred space,
Nose to nose,
Face to face;

Pelicans glide,
Bank on a salty, misty aerial tide,
The blanket of humidity,
It, like a layer of atmospheric pressure,
Wrings the waters from the sky,
In the brilliance of a solar heat,
In which the dimensions thrive,
The beaches of Exuma Infinite,
Into Jekyll Island tied,
In the spinning disk marked with God's fingerprints,
It just is...

...There is no how,
There is no why...

...As a Loggerhead lumbers into the tall grass,
On a high dune in the darkness,
We are here together,
For you have brought back the power of vision,
In these broken eyes.

"Modality Channels in the Material World"

Use the wind; the scent of fragrant purple flowers; the rustling, velvety leaves that give vocals to your angelic voice; stream in the breeze and reach my soul...

...Show me the foaming purple tides where the runoff from Diamas Regn filters through the shallows and is swallowed by the turquoise blue sea;

Seagulls overhead, dressed in quilted feathers of bright white streams of fire, these shooting stars arch across the cobalt night, wondrous lanterns, glorious displays of mystery;

Use the clay, the soil, stone; electricity; cloud; ocean, rivers and lakes; a thicket and individual trees I pass beneath dreaming of your face, your physicality as a baby, a toddler, a young girl, and older girl, a tween and a young teenager, a radiant young woman just before the accident took your physical life, in which you transitioned into your body of light;

I see you in the wind; feel you in the wind; call my name, my Precious Child; your Father is here no matter the challenge, no matter the hurdle, no matter the dimensions I struggle through to embrace you, bound in the material and physical world, but yearning higher into spirit, while you, in your body of light have the best of both worlds - in the glory of Heaven in your light body and also on the physical plain alongside your family in your body of light - there are channels most can't see; can't believe; cannot be. Yet we find the channels. We use the channels that bind us. We always have. We always will, my Little Girl. For we are the ones...

"Eyes Elsewhere (While She Is)"

It can be many things,
This elsewhere brings,
The shiny object that attracted distraction,
Forced the miss at the task at hand,
While rummaging in overreactions,
In the midst the loss of focus grand;

Or focused on the right thing,
This is what the elsewhere can bring,
You ask me to partake in trivial discussion,
While I am tending a bridge through the ether,
With spiritual constructions,
While you are heady, headlong in the headlines,
I haven't the time,
For my eyes are elsewhere,
In an elevated state,
Spending precious time with my beloved Daughter,
Yearning across the dimensions;

You may see me seemingly lost in thought,
You may see me seemingly talking to myself,
You may see me seemingly sitting alone,
You may see me seemingly without the companionship,
Of someone else;

Yet,
Just because you cannot see her,
Means not that she is not here,
Just because your prejudice prevents soul sight,
Means not this road we do not share;

Fear not,
For I am far from lost in thought,
For I am far from talking to myself,
For I am far from sitting alone,
For I am far from the companion I love best,
For my miracle is my Daughter,
Who laughs in the smile of the present tense.

"Spiritus Mycelium Autem Vitalia"

She is an ocean of abundance, full of life,
The most loveable person one can love,
She is life giving herself,
In all that she is and all that she was,
She is compelled of strong, living water,
Listen carefully to this one,
And the wisdom that she speaks,
For she has been groomed by the Highest Order,
And given the power,
And offers by desire,
To teach;

In the hush, I now know,
There are angels that have protected this home,
Sentries of humility hidden in garden flowers,
And ocean breezes that kissed her cheek,
Hour after hour,
For this soul, this soul is full of life,
She is living with full soul vision of sight,
Vitalia…

…She places her hands upon my brow,
And opens my crown to the mysteries of loving calm,
As I recognize her undeniable touch, somehow,
And expand my awareness just under her palm,
As she whispers,

"Daddy, Daddy, my Daddy, I am here,
I love you with all of my heart,
I have never left your side,
Daddy, walk with me under these Exuma stars,
For we are always together, we are."

And in my human condition,
The moments may seem fleeting,
Yet each build upon the path towards my ultimate transition,
With each daily meeting,
And we gently twine these immortal cords of light,
Like mycelium that support each other with substance of life,
We are Vitalia,
We are love itself,
We are together,
And stronger,
Than this temporary human shell...

...Your Daddy hears you, Honey,
Pull me through the grief,
For I re-awaken,
Each time you kiss my cheek,
Each time you kiss my cheek...

"Tightening the Sails (Into the Sky Mouth)"

I found this life's light trailing,
All of life assailing,
The wind curl into vicious eddies,
Dangerously prevailing;

I found my fingers failing,
My emotions railing,
The winds now walls of hurricanes...

...Tempting sailing;

But I am unafraid here,
In the harbor and it's barrier,
I have built a steady skiff,
The ship of life we share;

I pull the ropes and sheets lock cleats,
I bank across the angry sea,
I venture forth with courage leaning,
Into all that lies before me;

And you, you chart this steady course,
Into the sky mouth of a monstrous horse,
You, you are a fearless force,
You, my child, I trust you with my soul...

...Wherever we may go.

"Faith, A Sturdy Boat"

And as I trudge the tropical tundra,
The chop of unheralded waves,
Sweat stinging my eyes,
Covered in salt fragments,
Brave the ocean's dragon,
Colliding with the maelstrom,
Swallowing the swords of panic,
That eviscerate my throat,
Gasping for quality air,
In the smoldering fires emitting toxic smoke,
I arise and clasp the armor upon me,
Like a loose and cotton coat,
And strike out across the unknown,
These twenty hours of water road,
With my eyes affixed upon you,
In Faith, my sturdy boat.

"Swimming the Exuma"

A hundred dialects dare to gather,
Auroral weaving aerial effects,
In the coral haunts of the shallows,
Where the azure sky in the water reflects,
And I see your beautiful face,
Your golden hair,
That smile, Kayleigh, that smile,
Standing here before me,
In your black bikini,
In water up to your waist,
Compelling me to join you swimming,
A wink of the eye,
Pointing into the shoals of sea and sky and space,
Where the Loggerheads and the angels and the rainbows race;

Under these waters a mystery,
Cobalt blues and scarlet reds,
From the sea floor to the towers' heads,
The colonies thrive among the others,
Giving a mosaic effect;

And you ask me to follow,
And I, I somehow need no air,
As we swim the pure Exuma,
And it's ethereal atmosphere;

And the waves they feel like calming, silky breath,
As they embrace my skin,
And the hidden undersea beauty,
Unfolds as does the undersea wind,
Blowing in the currents here,
With moon and sun converged,
And although there is much to see...

...My eyes remain on her...

DAUGHTER VITALIA

"Its Accidental Scar"

Immersed in perpetual tragedy,
This sentence for the innocence condemned,
In the randomness of the arbitrary,
We find ourselves in who we really are,
What we have always known -

Brilliance, fidelity, love and dedication,
Exposed upon our fertile brows,
Sprout from the mark that blade has etched into us,
With its accidental scar;

Yet with purpose He has gifted us,
With purpose, the gold of intercession,
With purpose, a higher purpose,
And breathe I may from the chakras,
What fruitful fluid flows from the challis of sight,
Reinvigorate my resolve,
After this, in this life, yet is life,
There is nothing left to solve,
So I turn from this world, though tethered,
And raise my eyes to the next higher call,
On a much higher road,
Remembering,
With tears in His eyes, with purpose,
Firmly as He said...

..."Watch me turn this tragedy...

...Into gold."

"I Believe (Flowers of Faith)"

In all that I have experienced,
First hand,
I can only convey her miracles,
To the open minded and to the doubt in man,
Oh, shallow man,
Oh, shallow man,
Tucked so deeply within your self propulsion sheath,
While you stumble without knowledge,
I stand here though in the strain of grief,
In stand here with the strongest belief,
If anyone ever had an excuse to turn away,
In would be the likes of me,
But I did not and I will not,
For I lie within the heartbeat of her grace,
And she picks from the garden's gift,
That I grow for her each day,
These flowers, draped in sea petals,
These flowers of faith.

"Ceili Vitalia"

Never the world has met one such as your spirit,
(Your Father is so proud of you),
A beautiful dynamo wrapped into the life a gentle girl,
Your soul the ever dynamic, ever elastic beacon,
Enhanced by your physical presence,
(My Daughter, you are simply gorgeous),
Entrancing beauty transfixes the eyes in the crowds,
Encapsulated in that vibrant smile,
Breathtaking ocean blue eyes,
Accentuated by your long flaxen golden shiny hair,
As golden as a sunrise in a summer atmosphere,
That framed your tropical angular, stunning face,
With equatorial cheekbones,
And lips that lower the hurricane into a hush,
Vitalia,
Vitalia…

…Your Daddy waits for you at the garden gate,
A notebook filled with your future life's plans,
Left unfilled,
Yet he holds onto this leather bound book,
Even after you were physically killed,
As he hears your words,
And feels your presence,
Ceili,
Vitalia,
Amore Fati,
He knows,
He does not know…

"An Antenna"

Open my crown like an antenna,
Amplify our contact in the channel of sound,
In the channel of touch,
Where your gentle fingers are found,
Circling through my hair,
Delicately, tracing the framework of my crown,
Opening my soul from its fleshy shell,
To all possibility that lay outside of me,
That resonates all around,
Bringing my spirit into view of your soul,
Where our communications across the dimensions are effortless...

...And profound.

"The Voice of Vitalia"

As she exited the womb and heard my voice,
She turned her face towards me,
By comfort, by familiarity, by choice,
In love with her Father,
Deliberate, and only a few seconds old,
Dedicated, delicately poised;

And this song between us, virtue,
Ennobled in the tapestry of our souls,
This eternal voice of love,
Vital, constant, resilient, bold;

And as the seconds neared this tragic transition,
She listened for permission in my voice,
She wrapped in the chords of safety,
Finding final comfort in all that she had ever known,
That she is loved,
That she is liquid light of the purest gold;

And this song between us, virtue,
Ennobled in the tapestry of our souls,
This eternal voice of love,
Vital, constant, resilient, bold;

And as we walk now in different bodies,
She finds my wayward hand in each new day,
She shows me the pulse of the universe,
And the courageous beauty of the Diamas Regns,
As she speaks through the various channels,
Vitalia, this voice, in song, she prays,
That I may see through her eyes,
And then, in a flash, I could see her face…

…She was leading my eyes upward into outer space.

"Brunch on a Sandbar on the Moon with Daddy"

"See there, Daddy, I told you they would pass while we were here," she said,
Crossing through the moon's glow,
And where the spinning wheels of the Milky Way spread,
The whales of Exuma swam through the galaxy waves,
Mighty creatures explode through water,
Like fireworks in the sky,
That left a permanent impression upon the experience of the eye,
Knowing, that they, can fly,
Knowing, that they, like you, do not belong to this world,
And neither do I;

You with purple orchids braded into your flowing blonde hair,
And Loggerheads swimming beside you,
And gazing up to their Star of the Sea,
Their beloved, sacred Seer,
And rubbing gently against your light,
To remain closest to the brightest object in the night;

And the Russian tea biscuits and iced tea,
That we split apart into equal portions of three,
One for you,
One for the plate of love between us,
And one just for me,
These are my most cherished moments with you,
Adrift in our pink and white eternal, unbreakable cord of love,
A sandbar at the glistening mouth of Heaven,
Where we enjoy each other's eyes,
Where we meet for this moment, soul to soul,
And into the light, this light, we grow,
On our special beach when the moon is full.

"If You Could Walk With an Angel"

If you could walk with an angel,
Would you,
When given no other choice,
Would you press your ear to the wind,
To hear your child's voice,
Would you intend with devotion,
To trade in worldly noise,
To sit in the quiet stillness,
And rejoice...

...Of course you would...

If you could walk with an angel,
Why wouldn't you?
If your child's physical life was ended,
What would you do?
Would you sink in depression,
Many, many do,
Or would you rise with your angel,
And find your rage to continue...

....Of course you could...

If you could walk with an angel,
In a new configuration,
Would you embrace the glory,
Of this new situation,
Would you search the universe,
To hold your child's hand,
Not yet - no you don't, no you can't,
Unless you have been there,
There is no way to understand...

...But I do...

So I walk with an angel,

In a Father's faithful pursuit,
And I walk with my Daughter,
In her brilliant truth,
She is my Little Girl,
Transitioned in her youth,
And elevated angelically,
In her Higher Life renewed,
And with love in my spirit,
And love in her soul too,
We walk with each other...

...This is what we do.

"Fire Fields"

In my travels I came upon a magical field,
Acre after acre of a vibrant yield,
Flowers petal-ed in flame,
Burn and rise again,
These fields of glorious, glowing flowers,
Fill the air with a lovely scent,
For unlike a natural fire,
These are Heaven sent,
And build upon life in the burning,
And reach in a higher yearning,
A beautiful scene to behold,
The fire fields are a doorway,
These fire fields a threshold,
Into the interconnection of the souls.

"We Knew How To Do This…"

Organically, we knew, somehow, how to do this. I have no idea how, but when the accident happened we shifted catastrophically, but shifted nonetheless. We organically knew how to adjust through the worst tragedy into a new configuration with total faith and engagement among the four of us. We just knew how. It is hard to explain. But we are amazing. And we knew how to do this. Whatever this is. We knew, and then proved that life continues beyond the limits of our physical lives. You proved this emphatically. We just knew it and we were right. We trusted it with eyes closed and dicing into the unimaginable abyss of suffering as few suffer in human life. I don't know how but we knew how to do this. And we will know the next step and the step after. Somehow.

Obviously, I wish the accident had not happened. I would exchange a thousand lives to reverse this impact. However, it did happen. And now I am so grateful for your presence in both the physical world and Heaven, in your body of light, walking with your family pleasantly and full of life while giving us glimpses of that glorious Higher Life. It does not weigh you down to walk both places at once on this one singular road. It is not something you are not supposed to be doing. You are not lost. You are not stuck on a "loop." Your energy is not "left over." What rubbish. You are a guardian angel kissing me in the wind; cooing in the throat of a morning dove; lapping at my feet in gentle waves; speaking through every channel in the material world you can find; and talking very directly to us right into our faces with your eyes blazing blue and that big huge smile on your face with your golden hair blowing about majestically behind you. You are here. I am sure of it. I am here. You are sure of it. Let us walk.

"Illumination (For LeAnn and Catie, and Catie and Jack)"

The toll of passionate integration,
The tides that exchange in transition,
We bare the cross station by station,
And master the mystery of this mission,
We grace the cradle of creation,
With the triumph of a new vision,
We bridge the flesh and spirit nations,
No severance, no division,
Illumination…

…Rise…

"Kayleigh and the Angel Cosmos"

Flying through a kaleidoscope of vibrant liquid light,
Millions of smooth glassy pieces melted in the sunlight,
Awash in joy and effervescent delight,
Within the rainbow bands of oceans of the cosmos,
Where the angels in flight,
Bless their loved ones graciously,
In the twists and turns of life;

And Kayleigh knows the channels well,
And the name of every Exuma sea shell,
So focused and precise,
For every hug she offers us,
She gives embraces twice,
One of God's favorite angels,
In elevated heights,
She plots the course across the sea,
This wooden skiff, this vessel breathes,
Salty air and chop of waves,
Traveling through the angel cosmos,
And its sparks of scarlet sprites;

For she has spoken in God's name, rejoice,
For here is the life of eternity,
Alight in Kayleigh's Voice,
For she has conquered itself,
An early tragic death,
And teaches the mysteries of the cosmos,
In her gentle words expressed.

"Responsible To, But Not Responsible For..."

"Of course I feel responsible, Daddy, cause it happened to me. You would feel the same. I know. I didn't cause the accident, which is so true. I wasn't doing anything I wasn't supposed to be doing. I wasn't distracted. I didn't make a mistake. I had one intention - to cross the road to get my shoes and to come home. That was it. Then the accident, out of nowhere, in a perfectly horrible moment, just happened.

But I am responsible to lead now, though I am not responsible for the accident. And since it happened to me, since I was the one who transitioned, it's my job now and my chance to lead the family forward. You know I'm so good at it. I've always wanted to lead us and now I get to do that.

"I know, Daddy...

...I know."

"Intercession"

(i) Angelic Pulses of Light

It is a gift, unique in the awakened soul,
The act of intervening on behalf of another,
In the harmony and mystery of love enchanted,
A part of the exchange between God and his children,
They give total submission and humble sincerity to God,
An angelic pulse of eternal fire that lights up the beach…

…God gave us both the talent to write,
Now you need help writing in the material world,
Though you write all the time in spirit,
In the physical world I am the one who can intercede for you,
Use my hands and my mind and my heart,
I am your pen,
This,
This is the power of intercession;

(ii) The Vine

For He is the vine,
And we the flourished branches,
Inseparable, connected all,
In all He enhances,
Stand before eternity,
A mystical extension,
No death and no apprehension,
Can part the love between us;

(iii) Conversion of Voice

Help me convert the physical cues into spiritual cues,
Your voice has changed,
Your channels are not your vocal cords in your human flesh,
Yours are the wind,
The wind chimes,
The water,
The air,
The light,
Love,
Use every channel,
Teach me every channel,
In the universal language of light…

…As I visit you on the Exuma dunes,
Together counting the craters on the moon,
And watching the waves lap against the cosmos…

…Where the Loggerheads dance in the distant starlight womb.

"Waves of Cerulean* Song"

Bathed in the fragile texture of a green and bluish blend,
Where the sky and its sea converge,
Where there is no end,
Where the brilliant golden glaze on the waters,
Blinds the eye when morning extends,
And reaches through the darkness,
And with its light the night amends,
Brilliant in its song...

These waves of cerulean crash upon the door,
These waves of cerulean that lap upon this shore,
These waves of cerulean have gathered in the deep,
And washed into the turquoise shallows,
Where lonely parents weep,
And wash away each painful moment,
Each day the gathering grief,
She sends the healing warmth of the ocean...

...Each time the ocean breathes.

*Derivative of *caelum*, meaning "sky, heaven, atmosphere"

"Saoirse"

In that moment I shed the glory skins of my soul,
As all eyes strained upon the parent,
And found me on center stage,
Holding my child in this road,
Where I expelled deep bands of holy light,
In a horrible heartbroken groan,
And focused on her brilliant spirit,
And eclipsed all of our prior growth,
In that eternity of sixty seconds,
Focused like blinding light down a perfect tunnel,
That each of us could see in the other,
At either end…

…Each other.

"Angel Intercession"

They usher in a presence,
They convey an intention,
They speak in prayer tongues,
They inspire intercession,
They bring clarity,
To spiritual congestion,
They live in the sequence,
And breathe intervention,
In response;

They minister connection,
And set torches light the road,
They lay clues for our inspection,
On our footpath and exposed,
They offer this protection,
Connect Exuma and the soul,
And pronounce His essences,
Whether walking on water,
Or envisioned wrapped in buffalo robes;

Rise in the cradle,
Watchers of divinity,
They read the history of humanity,
And marvel at its simplicity,
They grab our attention,
And wrap us in felicity,
Spiritual warriors,
In dreams or in visions,
On beaches of infinity…

…Dispatched to call us into the eternity of now,
Where only then can we truly know,
The power of the immortal cord,
That binds and blends our souls.

"An Angel of the Highest Order"

It takes every bit of energy,
And more than all of my skills,
And I, in daily battle with rapturous grief,
For my child has been physically killed,
I swallow sorrow's thorny knife,
And choke on its furious blade,
And remember that deep in the fight,
The promise that I made,
Holding you in my arms,
As your last, young breath escaped...

...My Love...

...And in your miracle eyes,
And into the sunset the skies were filled,
With glistening souls like diamond beings,
To remind me that,
Though your physical body was killed,
Your soul it sings,
For you are alive,
Alive...

...And the Angels of the Highest Order converged,
And these Angels of the Highest Order wiped away my tears,
And leaned in as my heartbeat surged,
And whispered to me...

...That...

...You were one of theirs...

"The Infinite Endless"

Father, Father, peer through the air if this you can,
I know that you are still contained within the shell of a man,
Though I know you, and I know you very, very well,
If anyone can do this, Daddy, I will tell you,
You clearly understand –

As we go walking on this beach,
Just like the walks on a Georgia shore,
In my childhood the love was so deep,
As deep as the love beyond this Exuma door;

And into the Infinite Endless we go,
Traveling with me in the ascent of the astral,
Where the ocean speaks, unfurls its colors,
And wraps its light around our souls,
For into the Infinite Endless,
The source of all we dearly hold,
Take my hand, Daddy, in perfect trust,
And let go…

"Into the Ultraviolet"

Follow your eyes into the ultraviolet,
Hold them awake and wise,
Eyes opened wide,
And absorb the truest color of nature,
The bands of light in which the soul resides.

"Communion of Saints"

For those who have intended,
Bound in the light of immortal friendship,
Anamchara, Gloria, Exuma beach,
All blended in ascension,
Like the complex color wheels of oil paints,
Threaded on the canvas of the sky,
Commune with us, Saints,
And together with us…

…Rise.

"Pen Time"

In ascension of intended mind,
In comprehension of the meaning of time,
In intercession with my Daughter and the Divine,
We cross dimensions and blend and combine,
Together, together to write,
Sitting on your bed, my Little Girl,
Every night –

I offer you the gift to guide my hands,
As you use my vessel to scribe your plans,
I offer you perfect permission to stand,
In the big country of my soul with the chance,
To express yourself in artistic writing,
Sitting on your bed, with you, my Little Girl,
Nightly…

"Speed of God"

Cassiel, with his arms folded like golden calm,
With watchful eye bathing the cosmos, with its intricacies,
As it unfolds without the nature of his intervention,
Mindful of kings and saints,
With the speed of God's heartbeat,
Throwing spears with stardust tails into the night;

If there, over beyond the opaque salty clouds,
A Seventh Heaven there resides,
No matter the number and classes of angels,
That trip and trap the human mind,
All we need to know,
Just like we know there are stars,
All we need to know,
That angels…there are,
Angels of the highest presence,
And a High Order of angels,
In which mine holds her own;

God can do what God wants to do,
Yet He interacts with the physical world,
Sometimes through,
The direct intercession of His favorite souls,
Those who serve Him incorruptibly,
In the joy of love where the heartstrings grow,
She is finding the prettiest sea shells,
And placing them in my palms to hold,
Each of them a breathing star,
Pulsing the strobe of a living light of gold.

"Beach Angel"

Dragging myself across the barb-wired morning, sobbing,
Gutted with grief and torrents of tearful eyes,
I heard a voice so emotively familiar,
Call my eyes towards the tides,
And there, right there, standing before me,
In the flowing pink cords of sunrise...

...My Beach Angel,
My Daughter in gowns of silky light...

...With wings of quilted feathers of liquid life,
Flow from the calm between her shoulders,
Softly sparkle in a radiant vibration,
In the brilliant halo that holds her,
She is smiling for she sees that I see her,
In a burning bright white light,
That illuminates her facial features,
Her earthen blue eyes,
Her dynamic compassion,
And strings of opal petals weave into her flaxen blonde hair,
Glisten like diamonds as the warm windy atmosphere,
Swirls about her in a smoky prayer...

...And arching, glowing angel wings that flow behind her,
They suddenly dissolve into tiny rainbow translucent bubbles,
That lift upward unfolding and changing into...

...A million golden butterflies that disperse above her,
As her wing frames disappear,
Into a swarm of tiny golden monarchs,
They flutter about, filling the sky in every direction,
With pure joy,
And hope,
And love...

...And then, just as suddenly,
They magically fly back by the bundles,
Repositioning themselves into rebuilt arches,
Full and bountifully across her back,
Tucked into her golden blonde hair,
And radiating into the glowing wings of an angel...

...My Beach Angel,
My Daughter,
My Love.

"The Soul of the Sea"

Whales converse in poetic verse,
The porpoise through the surface burst,
Seagulls bark in rhythmic melody,
The sun sparks the salt crystals in the sea,
While on the beach,
Beachcomber beckons to speak,
Staring at his shoes,
Hoping for a moment of peace...

...While the ocean bares us its golden bands of turquoise blues...

"Daughter Ocean"

Daughter ocean,
Daughter sea,
Daughter moon,
Daughter, she....

...she is the world to me,
Physically killed in a tragedy,
Daughter ocean,
Daughter sea...

...And the grief it pulse and break,
Like the crash of wave after wave,
Nothing worse than this much aches,
I have to remind myself every day,
That your physical presence has been ripped away,
From me,
Daughter ocean,
Daughter sea,
Daughter midnight,
Dare to dream...

...As raw as pain can incinerate,
No more horrible for a parent than this fate,
And in each morning as I divorce from slumber,
And the first moments of the day pull me under,
I turn to you,
Daughter moon,
I turn to breathe,
My Daughter sea,
And you, you turn to me...

...As if fully submerged in the shallows on a coral reef...

...I feel your water arms all around me.

"Reluctant and Confident (A Flashback to Fifteen)

A subtle self-consciousness,
As your eyes drew gentler still,
In a hopeful yet sheepish manner,
Your face with a smile to fill,
In those moments as a teenager you questioned yourself,
You were humble, although this, you will,
Come bursting out with wistful laughter,
Heavier after,
You realize all you have built,
And concede to the looking glass,
An amazing woman returns the glance,
For never could these shoes be filled.

"In the Glory of that Final Chart"

A chart to cross space and time,
Where the sea meets the sky,
Where we meet in the eye,
Where our spirits are twined,
We find a magnificence unfold,
We find only in that perfection,
For there is no mystery left to learn,
No stone that is left to be turned,
No further lesson to surmise,
Where the sea meets the sky,
We walk hand in hand...

...Into the highest light.

"Sea Eagle"

We are the mighty osprey,
As free as the wind itself,
Perched in the cloud branches,
And illuminating the dimensions,
With stealth,
Lovely and loyal and sacrificially preset,
Like a phoenix who faces the prospects of death,
For family and faith,
There is nothing greater than this grace,
That I see in this osprey's eyes,
And lined on its salt water face..

...A sea eagle winged in glittering gray seeks solitude,
A gull of the Gods,
A soul of the ages,
We are the mighty osprey,
As we fly through these lives to higher lives,
To sky after sky,
Through all of our changes,
Written in the golden ink of unbreakable love.

"The Essence of an Angel"

This one, oh Lord, is more alive,
Than her brother, her mother and I combined,
That is the perfect essence of an angel,
When one so divine,
Transitions from life to life,
An elevation...

...So high, it seems,
That the stars themselves, now as low as sea shells,
Carpet the shallows of space and time,
Beneath her feet...

"This Pink Cord of Unbreakable Light"

I want to breathe in an ocean dream,
Burn away the flesh like sunrise steam,
That smokes upon the waters,
Where the spirit of the sea speaks to the soul...

...The Regns that hampered antiquity,
Fall upon my ocean throughout history,
Fall upon this ocean like a mystery...

...That we churn into gold...

...The sparkling rain screams,
Like a clutch of banshees sings,
Eroding with their beautiful torches,
Just about everything...

...Awaiting the clouds aloft to dissipate,
Awakened to the shrouds of light,
That warm the skin in the storm's promised wake,
I wake each morning to the first wretched thought,
How cruel this fate to wear on this every day...

...And so I breathe in an ocean's dream,
I absorb your energy,
As we blend in the love we together weave,
Into a pink cord of light tethered in eternity...

..."Oh, faithful this family,"
She whispered,
"Breathe the ocean, Daddy...

...Believe."

"A Galaxy of Sea Turtles II"

A million tiny teardrop sized glassy sea turtles,
All congregated into a magnificent body of light,
Your body of light,
Your body of life,
That radiates across the dimensions,
And illuminates, with hope, with faith, with love...

...The forbears of human night.

"Purple Sea Angel"

She, with blessings, abundance,
And in her palms, a glistening sea,
She wakes up the solar winds,
That have waned to a whisper inside of me,
She blows upon her open hand,
And the glitter lifts into a green and silver galaxy,
And swirls in the corner of our Creator's eye,
Like a perfect grain encapsulating a golden dream...

...She sings, laughing, bringing this to me,
A miracle, the likes the world rarely sees,
But only because the world is not awake,
And only because she and I, intuitively,
See what it is in these worlds,
We are meant to see...

..Lead me, Purple Angel,
Your Father sobs in a hurricane of grief,
Breathe me, Purple Angel,
My Daughter, you know what I need,
As we walk along this turquoise sea,
With its lavender sky draped in banks of aqua steam.

"The Visitation"

When the parapets, unguarded, are empty of sentiment,
When defenses lower and the conscience has lulled,
When the muscles retreat and scatter for shelter,
In the flanking hills of restless sleep,
Recuperating from the day's strains,
When the mind cannot dissect the problems in the logic,
I may,
Wish to rip off my skin,
And burn down the earth,
And rage against this fate,
Face down in the dirt,
And already crowned upon broken knees,
I beg,
Praying for signs,
Crying purple tears,
Praying in blue,
For a miracle to appear,
Only then is the dimension fully open,
Only then the field is ripe,
To receive a visit of truth,
A gift coming through that door,
And through my soul,
A visitation promised,
A visit, My Love, from you.

"Jekyll Exuma Threaded"

And so, following another storm of heartache, sobbing, distress, we sit here on the beach of Jekyll Island; me in my physical body and you in your body of light. We sit here now where once we sat here together both in our physical bodies, a Daddy and his Daughter enchanted by each other, and the sea, on an island of jungle, mystique, whitish sands and brownish blue waters; the beaches that stretched across your childhood, your life; the sun a steady guide to relaxation, family, love and light. As you would say, "the spirit of the sea speaks to the soul."

So here we are and I am grateful amidst the Diamas Regn; amidst the constant grief and the unquenchable storms of heartache that rifle through my soul each second of each day since the accident stripped you of your physical being at the young age of fifteen.

As you instructed, I came back here. I sit here to meditate and close my eyes. You resonate so strongly here, here on this beach where we spent two weeks together, the four of us, Mommy, Daddy, your little Brother, our Girl, just before returning home to Cleveland, and suffering the most horrific tragedy of your physical death in an innocent car accident.

"Exuma Infinite, Daddy," you said, "close your eyes. We are going to blend the two plains. Merge Jekyll Island, Georgia, in the physical world where you are contained in your human state, with that of the spiritual world of Heaven at Ceili Cay, Exuma Infinite, where I light up the worlds in my spiritual body. I am the bridge, Daddy, me and God, for He has allowed me, as you know, to remain with you as an intercessor, guiding my loves, my sweet little Brother and my wonderful Parents forward as a family of four. I am so grateful. I get to, in my spiritual body of freedom, be in the glory of Heaven in Exuma Infinite while also being in the physical dimension in my body of light with you on this physical plain. How amazing is my life? Close your eyes, Daddy, and see my face. I want you to see what I see. I want to show you Exuma Infinite. I want you to come there with me while we are also sitting here on the sand of Jekyll Island. You've learned on our many journeys that it takes concentration to travel, but it is not impossible. For you are graced with intuition, and are already between both worlds. I love that we spend our time together like this. It is so amazing."

That it is, my Child. I close my eyes. I bring intention. I breathe devotion. I bring the humble request to God to remain tethered in my human flesh while traveling also with you to Exuma Infinite, on an island you christened, "Ceili Cay," as God permits, as God allows, as God wills us to do, as God wishes the world would do more often. We do. We know. We are together, not just after I physically die, but now, albeit in different body types. We are together.

The merging, it is truth that blends here. Brown and turquoise waters. Purple and blue skies. Whitish sand and pure white powdery sand. The seas flood the heavens.

"Daddy, what you will find is that Exuma Infinite was here all along on Jekyll Island where we together sit."

"Celestial Angelic Infrasound*"

And she, with celestial innovation,
And endless love, the fuel and motivation,
To embrace and encourage her family;

She is using every law of nature,
Every law of the Heavens,
To evolve communication,
She is speaking through the flowers and the leaves,
And the wind that cups the ocean's break,
Through soul waves and light waves and sound waves,
To build a bridge across the breach,
And I turn my attention suddenly,
As the skin hears her words...

...It resonates;

And though her lovely voice sometimes strums below my audibility,
With limited hearing in the lower frequencies,
Her angelic vocalization,
In a sacred manner and moored in secrecy,
Kisses my ears and the senses lift,
Feeling her words as the vibrations shift,
And my body receives her message,
In this highest intensity...

...Of love;

They say the beauty of this sound wave,
The ability, without dissipation, to move around,
To maneuver obstacles where they are found,
Is an immutable characteristic of the soul,
Measured and mastered by this one,
Sitting beside me in harmonious glow;

My Child, for whom my grieving heart longs,
If in breath I can this life slow,
She crosses the threshold of infrasound,
As she shouts loudly in laughter towards my ear,
Intentionally,
In the whispers that penetrate the air,
I hear the most familiar, lovely voice,
And feel her gentle touch,
As she holds me close and says,

"Daddy, I am right here...Daddy...

...I love you so much!"

* *Always present, always reaching out to us; sometimes we hear her voice audibly above the infrasound, yet when we do not hear her, our skin still feels her words.*

"We Do It Differently"

But we do it,
With raw courage,
No matter what,
For we always do...

...We move forward,
Find each other where we are,
In who we are,
And we fight forward kicking and screaming,
If we must,
And now in this place in our history,
We must...

...At age five it was different than nine,
And ten different than twelve,
And twelve a different equation than fifteen,
Yet now the equation is much more complex,
But an equation nonetheless,
We do it differently,
But we find each other,
No matter what.

"A Sky Door Tucked In Rainbow Thunder"

And into the harvest of nighttime I bow,
As the spirited wind awoke,
Amethyst clouds, indigo smoky shrouds,
Emerald green streaks of smoke,
Auburn and orange apprehension,
A golden halo erupts in the thunder tension,
Just as the humidity chokes...

...And collapses in on itself...

...We were there faithfully holding hands;

Have you ever watched the rain as it dances in flames,
Millions of crystals, charged lightning, that lights up our souls,
And lights up the tears in our eyes,
And illuminates this road,
As this road lifts into a tired rainbow burnt sky...

...For no human condition can understand,
(Little hints along the way),
Until the light body press the skin,
Filling the pores with sparkles of endlessness,
Glowing freedom droplets of eternity,
That collect by the millions,
And web into a tapestry of soul fabric,
As the physical life wears thin,
Until what becomes abound is that which was...

...Contained within;

She said, "Daddy, do you hear that sound, that sound in the wind?"

She grasped firmly my soar and achy palm,
(Hush),
And kissed my cheek,
Encouraged my calm,
(Silence...ssshhh),
She sighed, smiled deeply before she continued to speak,

"God is calling, Daddy," she said,
And pointed into the heather blush of wind,
That came to unleash itself in every direction at once,
Circling me in a perfect peace,
A thousand shades of vibrant colors,
That brought me to my knees,
Where she, too, kneeled reverently,
Before the Lord,
An angel of the Highest Order,
Packed so gently within my child,
Always loyally and loudly in my corner,
Who shook my soul loose from this frame,
In which it was moored,
Staring into the eyes of God together,
Kayleigh, Kayleigh...

...This door,
Ornate with filigree dreams of Heaven?

...We have been here before,
We have been here before...

"Stepping Out of the Skiff"

Stepping out into the acrid ocean air,
And into the turquoise water, velvety oil painting daydreams,
I go,
Ankle deep, barefoot, holding the skiff steady in the shallows,
Yet firmly the weight of its hull is creased into the white sand,
The sands of my soul,
The salty air of my soul,
The familiar of all that I have forgotten that I know;

She waits, standing on the dry sand, on a plain in a dimension,
It merges from water to land, from sea to sky,
From hand to hand,
The wind blows her long blonde hair,
She is radiant, standing in a loose fitting yellow tank top,
With black shorts, barefoot as well,
Her toes anchored in the dune;

We, in the other, have awaited this day with awe,
With excitement,
With utter disregard for the limitations of human life,
And I have missed her so in her physical form,
Yet have walked with her in her body of light,
Ever since her physical death,
On that horrible accident night,
I cry...

...These are tears of joy for I finally see,
The world that she wanted me to see,
As she took her final breath,
As she entered the Higher Life upon physical death,
Staring down the path of perfect light,
Calling to me as she transitioned,
"Do you see it, Daddy?
Do you see it?"

And now I, too,
See the panoramic vision of Exuma Infinite,
It releases at my feet as I step over the threshold,
From water to land,
From sky to sea,
From hand to hand,
And step before my daughter in our eternity,
Again, at last, in the same incarnation,
The same bodies of light,
A Daddy and his Daughter,
In heavenly Exuma,
Where she has prepared this destination,
Across the span of my life.

"We Walk in Water"

Barefoot, and with intention, I walked into the water, it, shimmering opal and wrapped in turquoise dreams; rising over my knees, my stomach, into chest deep gentle waves lapping against my skin, skin that reacts to the dislocation, the warmth of the sea contrasted with the heat in the air and the streams of light in the breeze; I go in here knowing with whom I swim, with whom I venture, my companion, my Little Girl;

I hear your tiny splashes beside me, as the water ripples out from your skinny legs that move through the shallows, until the silence comes; glancing to my right, inches from my shoulder, you are here, standing almost as tall as your Father, with long flowing silky blonde hair blowing in the breeze behind you, deep blue ocean eyes shining, and a smile that rises on your face like a field of wild flowers basking in a perfect sun;

You bump my shoulder with yours and let out a little laugh, humbled and happy, excited and grateful to go swimming with your Father; and I, equally excited, feel the range of emotion flutter within me, including nervousness, fear, joy, courage, faith; we have come here to swim in Exuma; we have intended and devoted this time, time we engage in constantly across the veil, blending in the dimensions, that no physical death can prevent;

So we walk in water and stand in the tides in this crystal clear sea, with rays at our feet gliding on the breeze, and tropical fish swimming and darting and playing with us; and so we walk in water, as I look into your eyes and know it is time, and, with no conscious thought of breath, while trusting the glowing angelic light that radiates in your eyes, we fully submerge into the living light of water to go explore the heavenly contours of an endless, deeply vibrant, rainbow coral reef.

"The Continue"

...How important to acknowledge, after all of these storms, of Saturn and Jupiter, that churn across the face of Earth, within me, without me, beyond our solar winds and the chiming tones of the moons fully abloom, in the star fields and the ocean nebula where the space whales and the Loggerhead splash in the slipstream, that the Diamas Regns have two interdependent, yet interconnected faces...

...Because, simply, the immense electrical storm of grief itself is an inverse window into an endless abundance of brilliant eternal love between us...

...And thus, logic bend, shadows melt, and the light of living water emerges to always find us breathing in the oceans of eternity.

www.ingramcontent.com/pod-product-compliance
Lightning Source LLC
Chambersburg PA
CBHW011140290426
44108CB00020B/2694